Buddhism and Immortality

The Ingersoll Lecture, 1908

BUDDHISM
AND IMMORTALITY

BY

WILLIAM STURGIS BIGELOW

BOSTON AND NEW YORK
HOUGHTON MIFFLIN COMPANY
The Riverside Press, Cambridge
1908

THE INGERSOLL LECTURESHIP

Extract from the will of Miss Caroline Haskell Ingersoll, who died in Keene, County of Cheshire, New Hampshire, Jan. 26, 1893.

First. In carrying out the wishes of my late beloved father, George Goldthwait Ingersoll, as declared by him in his last will and testament, I give and bequeath to Harvard University in Cambridge, Mass., where my late father was graduated, and which he always held in love and honor, the sum of Five thousand dollars ($5,000) as a fund for the establishment of a Lectureship on a plan somewhat similar to that of the Dudleian lecture, that is —one lecture to be delivered each year, on any convenient day between the last day of May and the first day of December, on this subject, "the Immortality of Man," said lecture not to form a part of the usual college course, nor to be delivered by any Professor or Tutor as part of his usual routine of instruction, though any such Professor or Tutor may be appointed to such service. The choice of said lecturer is not to be limited to any one religious denomination, nor to any one profession, but may be that of either clergyman or layman, the appointment to take place at least six months before the delivery of said lecture. The above sum to be safely invested and three fourths of the annual interest thereof to be paid to the lecturer for his services and the remaining fourth to be expended in the publishment and gratuitous distribution of the lecture, a copy of which is always to be furnished by the lecturer for such purpose. The same lecture to be named and known as "the Ingersoll lecture on the Immortality of Man."

BUDDHISM AND
IMMORTALITY

BUDDHISM
AND
IMMORTALITY

THE view of the Immortality of Man which I have the privilege of stating is, broadly speaking, that of the Buddhist religion. But Buddhism, like many other great religions, is divided into main churches and subdivided into sects: and we find conspicuously two broad divisions, commonly called Northern and Southern Buddhism, — the former having its recognized centre in the north of India, in Nepaul; the latter in Ceylon. The history, the significance, and the relations of these two divisions consti-

tute a vast field of study, into which
we cannot attempt to enter to-night.

What I have to say relates primarily
to the Northern or Nepaulese Buddhism, and more especially to the doctrines of the two closely allied sects
which represent that form of Buddhism
in Japan. These sects are known respectively as the Tendai and the Shingon. The whole of Northern Buddhism is closely allied to Brahminism,
with which it is historically directly
connected. There is a close resemblance in the tenets and doctrines of
the two religions, even in their super-
ficial aspects; and the more deeply
they are studied, the closer is the connection found to be. The forms of religious service are essentially the same
in both; and even in Japan to-day the

greater part of the Shingon and Tendai ritual is not in Japanese but in Sanscrit, and is identical with that which has been in use in India since before the time of Buddha,—so long before, in fact, that there is no historic record of its origin, and there is reason to believe that it antedates written history altogether. It certainly appears to be the oldest ritual now in actual use in the world. A similar correspondence between India and Japan is found to hold essentially good in regard to those special presentations or aspects of the great central force of the universe, which are embodied in anthropomorphic forms and recognized as separate deities.

It may be said in passing, that for the understanding of such a vast and

intricate system of thought, or even
of so small a part of it as we have to
consider here, the student handicaps
himself with needless difficulties if he
begins by classifying it under some such
customary heading as Pantheism, Poly-
theism, Monotheism, Materialism,
Idealism, and the like. We all carry
in our intellectual pockets a quantity of
gummed labels bearing the names of
such familiar categories, which we are
ready to attach to any new packet of
documents, however large, after exam-
ining the first one or two, and we then
expect to find that all the rest fit exactly into the Procrustean limits that
we habitually associate with that particular title. Whereas in the present
case the exact contrary is the fact; and
we find, on the one hand, that there

is ample room to attach almost every label that the mind of man has conceived; and, on the other, that each one is by itself inadequate.

Starting, therefore, without prejudice of any sort, I am going to try to set before you, in such brief outline as the allotted time allows, an epitome or digest of the teaching of these two Buddhist sects, the Tendai and the Shingon, in regard to the special subject to consider which this lectureship has been established,— the Immortality of Man. Part of what I have to say is of such elementary simplicity that I almost apologize for saying it, and indeed only do so to be sure that we start together. Part, again, though less simple, is familiar doctrine that may be heard here in the West in any lecture room or from any pulpit. And part, again, lies so remote from our ordinary Occidental habits of thought that I shall hold myself fortunate if I can succeed in making it intelligible.

The generous founder of this annual lecture chose the title well, in assuming the existence of something called man, and restricting the discussion to the question of how long that something lasts. Consciously or unconsciously, we all make the same assumption ; for it has been well said that "to doubt our own existence is to call in question the very existence of our doubt." In this attitude we have the support alike of the oldest religion and the newest science ; for Poincaré, in his latest scientific work, after discussing in detail the theories of force and matter and motion, of electricity and light and ether, sums up the state of the most modern knowledge in these concise words, — "Something exists."

However reckless and extravagant this statement may seem, let us accept it provisionally, and further, for convenience, let us give this something a name. Let us provisionally call it ourselves, — you and I, — *I* to each one of us, — and see what are some of the most obvious things to be said about it. What do we mean by it? What did Descartes mean by it when he said : "I think, — therefore I am"; and thereby implied the inevitable correlative: "I do not think, — therefore I am not"? What is the " I "? What is the "thought"? Are they the same thing or different things? Can either exist without the other?

Let us consider for a moment the ordinary popular view. According to this, man is a compound of a material and tangible part called the body and an immaterial and intangible part called the soul.

The facts about the body are simple, obvious, and familiar. Its existence is as certain as that of the rest of the material universe, and, except during life, it obeys the same laws. This is a fact of observation like any other; for instance, like the fact that fire burns or that water runs down hill.

The case of the soul is less simple. Being invisible and intangible, its existence is commonly assumed on two grounds. First, by inference, through its apparent effects. Second, by what we call self-consciousness. Under the head of effects we recognize, as most obvious, the formation and maintenance of unstable chemical compounds not formed by inorganic matter, and the building up of these compounds through intermediate stages of structure into a coöperative organism acting as an individual until death, when it ceases to act as a unit and disintegrates like any other unstable chemical product. The very fact of death, therefore, is evidence of the existence of something besides inorganic matter during life.

Secondly, as regards self-consciousness. We are all, as we familiarly say, conscious of our own existence. Under this statement we habitually include, in more or less confusion, several distinct elements.

First, the existence of our material bodies as objects of sensory perception, like any other material objects, such as chairs, tables, or other peoples' bodies, the only essential limitation being that no sensory organ can perceive itself. The eye sees the hand, but the eye does not see itself. To suppose it could would be a contradiction in terms, for normal sensation implies disturbance of a normal equilibrium by an external stimulus.

Second, of certain sensations, pleasurable or painful, originating not outside but inside the body itself.

Third, of certain disturbances apparently not of material origin, that we classify as passions or emotions.

Fourth, of what we call aptitudes and their opposites.

Fifth, of desires or inclinations and their opposites.

Lastly, of something of a wholly different character, consciously closer to the centre than anything else, and differing from the other forms in being the only form of consciousness to which we are not passive. This we call will. We say, I feel sensation, pain, or emotion; but we never say, I feel my will. It is always subjective and active.

These are the main facts, simply stated, in the commonest terms of daily life. Let us look at them at a different angle. I once asked Dr. Holmes, toward the end of his life, the question,

"What is a man?" He answered, without hesitation, "A series of states of consciousness."

The word "series" introduces the element of time, the relation of which to states of consciousness is empirical and not essential. Broadly speaking, certain states of consciousness associated directly or indirectly with matter occur in sequence in every-day human experience, but the same states may occur simultaneously under exceptional circumstances. It is well known that in the sudden presence of imminent and apparently certain death, the accumulated states of consciousness of a lifetime sometimes revive simultaneously in a single flash. The events of the whole past are seen down to the most minute and remote details, like a landscape under a flash of lightning. Dr. Hòlmes himself had had this experience on one occasion, just before losing consciousness altogether while drowning, and the memory of the occurrence persisted after resuscitation. But if, in answering my question, he had left out the one word "series," Dr. Holmes's definition would have been identical with that of Buddhism, which is this, —"A man consists of states of consciousness."

Now, from this point of view, the whole question of the Immortality of Man is bound up with the question of the persistence of these states. This persistence depends on their character and origin. Some may persist longer than others. The states of consciousness that we recognize in every action of daily life are obviously divisible into two classes, namely, those that originate from without and those that originate from within. The first are conditioned by space and time, the latter are not.

Let us take a homely illustration, the simpler the better. Each of you, let us say, had breakfast this morning. While you were eating it you were conscious of it, how it looked and tasted, and these states of consciousness were imposed on your minds from the outside by the action of matter on matter, —the matter of the breakfast on the matter of your nerves of sight and taste. This action is as constant as any other purely mechanical action, and if your sensory and nervous machinery is in normal running order, the resulting

states of consciousness are as constant
as the cause that produces them. All
these forms of consciousness, I repeat,
were imposed on your minds from without in the form of distinct sensations,
as we call them, sensations existing at
that particular time and place.

Again, you are conscious of being in
this hall to-night. As before, this consciousness is imposed on your minds
from without in the form of distinct
sensations existing at this particular
time and place. You see the hall and
the audience exactly as you saw your
breakfast-room and your breakfast.

Now, think, for a moment, of your
breakfasts. Where and when is that
thought? Is it here and now, or there
and then? Plainly it is here and now,
because you are here, now, and it is

your thought. Equally plainly it is there and then, or it would not be the thought of this morning's breakfast. It is therefore both. Now a state of consciousness conditioned by two mutually exclusive opposites is unconditioned by either. In other words, your thought is unconditioned by space and time.

By what, then, is it conditioned? The answer is as important as it is obvious. It is conditioned by your will, —the act of volition that calls the thought of the breakfast into being, and not by the direct sensory impressions, whose forms and sum it reproduces. Herein lies the fundamental difference between the consciousness of the breakfast as you eat it, and the consciousness of it that you, being in another place, create by an act of will twelve hours afterward.

This second state of consciousness is conditioned only by the will, and we can make it what we choose. If our mental machinery is in good working order, we can recall the breakfast exactly as it was. This we call memory. Or, if we like, we can increase or diminish or alter it in any particular. For coffee and rolls, we may substitute ortolans and peacocks' tongues, and so on. There is no limit to it. This we call imagination; and what I want to emphasize is that memory and imagination are identical in being states of consciousness produced by the will, and differ only in the closeness of their correspondence with antecedent states.

Here, then, at the outset are two

opposite ways in which states of consciousness may be produced. First, from without, by matter acting on matter, either through contact, direct or indirect, or by means of vibrations, such as those of sound and light. This we may call, for convenience, the sensory origin of consciousness, since it involves direct relation through the senses with the great machinery of external nature,— machinery which goes at its own rate and in its own way, and acts as a stimulus to consciousness on the one hand and a pendulum or balance wheel to it on the other. Second, from within, by the action of the will.

Is there a third way? Obviously there is. Suppose we disconnect the pendulum of material nature from one end of the machine and the guiding motive power of the will from the other, the wheels will keep on turning for a time by their own momentum, and states of consciousness will ensue which are apparently spontaneous. The most familiar instance of this is in common dreams. Such states of consciousness, having neither guide on the one hand nor check on the other, are usually dislocated and confused, but in this respect there is, of course, a vast range of difference. A dream may be, and commonly is, incoherent to the point of grotesqueness. It may be anything from that up to a logical continuous sequence, as distinct and vivid as a waking reality. In a well-known and often cited case, such a sequence continued night after night in the form of a separate dream-life, with its own events and incidents, until the dreamer found himself literally unable to tell which of the two alternate lives he was leading was the real one. Each had its orderly succession of days and nights, and going to sleep in one meant waking up in the other. Each was real while it lasted, the other being the dream until he came back to it, when the conditions were again reversed. It is well to bear this case in mind as a good illustration of an important, though elementary, fact, namely, that every complete state of consciousness is real to itself, and unreal to other states.

We have, then, broadly speaking, three separate and definite ways in which states of consciousness may originate,—one external, and two internal; namely, through the senses, by the will, and spontaneously. The first, in a normal organism,—and we are not considering here any pathological conditions whatever,—is as regular and invariable as the order of external nature, on which it is based. The second conforms to external nature or deviates from it, as we choose. When it conforms, we call it memory. When it deviates, we call it imagination. The third is generally irregular, and depends on the momentum or impetus of the thinking machinery itself.

I have spoken so far of external and internal stimuli as exciting consciousness, and most of you have accepted these terms without giving them a second thought. Internal and external,

subjective and objective, ego and non-
ego, self and the rest of the universe,
— these categories are not only familiar, but from our western point of
view fundamental, and represent the
first great obvious distinction which at
once underlies and dominates most, if
not all, of our religious, philosophical,
and scientific thought. Consciously or
unconsciously, we habitually think of
ourselves and the universe in those
terms.

Let us examine them a little more
closely. Internal and external — external to what?

Certainly, not external to consciousness, in the Buddhist view, for they *are*
consciousness, and nothing else. To
say that they are external to it is a contradiction in terms. They exist only in

consciousness. If they are external to it, they cease to exist.

External to the body, then? This is more like it. The body is a material object; and whatever else it may be in its relation to the phenomena of its own organic life, it is itself matter in its relation to other matter.

What, then, do we mean by matter as we ordinarily understand the word? For practical purposes we commonly mean aggregations of centres of vibration whose rate lies between the lowest infra-red and the highest ultra-violet which are the normal working limits of our senses.

What are the simplest and most obvious characteristics of such matter, essential conditions of its existence by virtue of which it is matter? There are of course two, time and space. This is a commonplace. Yet it is of fundamental importance in this connection. For if, as I have tried to show you, certain states of consciousness, namely, the mechanical or sensory forms, have their origin in the action of matter on matter, then those states of consciousness will necessarily be subject in form to the two conditions of which I have just spoken.

This point is fundamental and vital. It is the turning-point on which the whole question of immortality hinges. Matter is conditioned by space and time. Direct sensory consciousness, being based on matter, is necessarily equally so conditioned. But states of consciousness not based on matter are not.

Now, the space and time relations of matter may be summed up in one word, separateness; those of conscious-ness in the opposite term, unity.

This seems too obvious to be worth stating. One chair is separate from another chair, one tree from another tree, one animal body from another animal body, — nor can you, by any means, make two into one. But with consciousness the exact contrary is true. Unity, not separateness, is the essential characteristic. Two men can-not sit in the same chair at the same time, but any number of men can think of the same chair at the same time. This seems a proposition of childish simplicity, and so it is, but it is the turning-point of the whole matter. I repeat, the essential characteristic of

matter is separateness. That of consciousness is unity. You cannot make
two chairs one. You cannot make the
consciousness of a chair anything but
one, no matter how many minds it occurs in. A proof of this last proposition, if proof were needed, is in the
use of language. You speak of a chair
to your neighbor. The word corre-
sponds to a definite state of consciousness in you which you want to excite in
him. If the word chair fails to do so, if
it excites a different state, or none, language is useless. Human intercourse
is based on the assumption that states
of consciousness, whether called up
by the arbitrary signal of a word or by
direct sensory impressions, are constant in every mind, and identical
in all minds. If it were not so, we

should be incontinently reduced to chaos.

So far we have dealt with states of consciousness as external and internal to the body. But how about the body itself? We have considered it as the vehicle or medium of transmission of mechanical stimuli from external sources to the conscious centre, which for convenience we have regarded as a sort of dial or indicator hung midway between the senses on the one hand and the will on the other. It is like the dial of a watch. The hands go at a definite rate exactly in time with the movements of the physical universe. That is sensory consciousness. But you can set them anywhere you like by rotating the appropriate knob. That is volitional consciousness. We have classed such sensory stimuli as external. But how shall we class stimuli that arise within the body itself? How about physical pain?

The case here is essentially identical with that of other sensory stimuli. You touch a knife. This is ordinary sensation. You cut your finger with it. Pain ensues. Either case is an instance of the impact of matter on matter,— the matter of the knife on the matter of your nervous terminations. The pain lasts more or less till the cut is well, the local disturbances of inflammation and repair still acting directly on the nerves of sensation, the same nerves through which both the touch and the cut were originally felt. The practical difference is that the pain is a danger signal. It shows that something

is wrong. That something may be a
cut, or the grating of a rheumatic joint,
or a neuralgic pain, but in every case
something is wrong. When a pain is
due to external injury, natural selection fosters its avoidance. Avoiding
pain means avoiding injury. Pain is
therefore, primarily, an element in the
conservation of the life of the individual, and therefore of the species, in the
presence of outside attacks, and it is to
be regarded as in this respect like any
other element in the process of natural
selection.

In this connection the following
stages are gone through:—

1. Animals who feel pain and avoid
it, thereby avoiding injury, tend to
be preserved by natural selection, as
against those who do not.

2. This habitual action of avoidance becomes reflex by habit, the withdrawal of a hand when pricked or burnt finally becoming automatic, and accomplished by a short circuit of the nervous telegraph wires without the intervention of consciousness.

3. In natural selection, as elsewhere, an ounce of prevention is worth a pound of cure, and the recognition and avoidance of pain as it occurs is amplified, still by natural selection, into recognition and avoidance of the source of pain as it approaches. And, by association rendered keen by inherited experience, the pain itself is in a measure anticipated, this anticipation being associated with the simultaneous desire to escape from it; and the combination of these two forms of con-

sciousness, like two metals fused into an alloy, in which neither is recognizable, produces what appears to be a new and wholly different form, which we classify as an emotion and call fear.

The other emotions have a similar origin. Anger, for example, is the combination of the recognition of approaching danger and the desire to repel it. I need not multiply instances to suggest to you that all the so-called lower passions and emotions are nothing but the accumulated effects of natural selection acting on single cases in favor of the conservation of the species, this action being favored and aided by the tendency of habitual action to become reflex. In this latter element lies their danger as well as their advantage. In a perfect organism they are absolutely

under the control of the will, which
is another way of saying that many of
them cease to exist.

These passions and emotions are
transmitted in accordance with another
law stated by Darwin, namely, that
the traits most sure to be inherited are
those which have been inherited longest, they being necessarily most directly
concerned with the persistence of the
type.

First in this classification comes the
need of safety; then of food. Both
these are the immediate needs of the
individual, and are therefore selfish,
centripetal, and exclusive.

Then come the multiform needs
connected with reproduction. These
are of two kinds, those connected with
the individual and those connected

with offspring. The former are, like
the need of safety and food, essentially
centripetal and selfish, though capable
of expansion. The latter are centrifugal, altruistic, and inclusive.

From the need of food, the need of
safety, and the individual interests connected with reproduction spring the
selfish lower emotions, such as anger,
hate, fear, jealousy.

The unselfish forms of love, especially of parental love, by a mere expansion of terms become charity and
altruism, and later by admixture of
other elements, such as imagination
and desire, become hope and faith. Ma-
ternal love is the source and origin of
all human virtues. This is not a figure
of speech. It is a fact of evolution.

Desire is the momentum of a checked

reflex.   Aptitudes are reflexes of slightly greater complexity, and as a rule not concerned directly with type preservation.   We say that a boy has an aptitude for music, but not an aptitude for eating.

So we may for convenience add another to our list of the forms of consciousness. We began with the sensory impressions in their five familiar forms. We added sensations of pleasure and pain arising within the body itself. We then saw that certain reactions to these impressions concerned in the preservation of the type were filtered out and fostered by natural selection, emphasized and strengthened by habit and its consequent reflexes, till their origin was for the most part lost to view, and they reappeared in the form

of abstract passions, emotions, aptitudes, etc., forms of consciousness so
remote from that from which they
sprang that they are almost unrecog-
nizable in their disguise.

So far we have been concerned only
with the ordinary experience of human
life as everybody knows it, and the
count up to this point is essentially
complete.

Is there anything else?

I have again and again referred to
the will, and you have understood me
without a moment's hesitation. This
will is a part of the normal consciousness of each one of you, yet it is
neither a part of sensation nor emotion, but on the contrary is capable of
dominating both.

What is it? Ask your own con-

sciousness. Sensations originate outside and inside the body; emotions,
inside. But the will is deeper than
either, and they are both objective to it.
We cannot classify it with anything
else. We cannot describe it in terms
of any other form of consciousness.
We are conscious through our bodies
and of our bodies, but the consciousness of the will is direct. We cannot
separate ourselves from it. We cannot stand off and examine it. We
cannot modify it by anything else. It
itself modifies everything within its
scope. Other forms of consciousness
are objective in their relation to it, but
it is never objective to them. It may
be overpowered by sensations, emotions, or passions, through its own
weakness or their strength. It often is.

But its attitude towards them, whether
resisting or directing them, is always
essentially and necessarily active. It
exists in no other form than the subjective form. It is inconceivable in any
other form. If it is not active, it is
not will. There is nothing in our consciousness deeper. It underlies and
overlies and permeates all other forms,
and, moreover,—what is of immea-
surably more importance,—it can, if
need be, *create them*. This last is the
central fact to which all that I have
said leads up. Fully to realize this is to
hold the key to immortality. Will is
the assertion of a form of consciousness from the centre outward. When
this is opposed by another form of
consciousness, intruding from the cir-
cumference inward, we recognize a hin-

drance to the free action of the will, and we talk of "necessity." But such intrusive forms are, as we have seen, ultimately and essentially of material origin. They come from or through the body,—the material, separate personality. If it were not for these, the will would act freely. The separate personal consciousness with its off-shoots is therefore the only obstacle to complete freedom of the will. Complete freedom of the will is complete freedom of consciousness, and complete freedom of consciousness from the habitual and empirical limitations of personality is complete freedom of the will. The terms are interchangeable. The only will that is not free is the personal will.

Descartes said, "I think, therefore

I am." It is an imperfect formula at
best, but it would have been a better
statement had he said, "I am conscious, therefore I am"; and best of all
had he said, " I will, therefore I am."

Now, is there anything more? How
about the "self"? How about the so-
called character? Is there not a separate
"self" back of it all,—a "self" that
feels and wills, but is neither feeling
nor volition, any more than the finger
is the pin that pricks it or the nervous
stimulus that moves it? Surely it would
seem there must be. Surely the existence of such a separate self would seem
to be the basis of all human actions.
Even at the beginning of this lecture,
our starting-point was to assume that
"something exists," and provisionally
to call that something ourselves.

What do we mean by the "self"? Obviously it is a limitation of some sort. What limits it? What shuts off the self from the rest of the universe? We are so small, the universe is so great, we say. Yet all we know of the universe is inside our heads. Are our heads, then, of cosmic dimensions? Or is the universe smaller than it seems? There is an inconsistency here somewhere. If the universe will go into a man's head, what is there about the man that is smaller than the universe?

Put in this way, the question answers itself. The man's material body is smaller, and that is the only thing about him that is. His mind, that is, his consciousness, is larger, and, what is more, it is indefinitely larger. It could take in a dozen universes, or a million, as easily as one. Consciousness has no dimensions.

But, you may say, if a man consists of states of consciousness, what, then, are the limitations of the "self"? If these states of consciousness may include the universe, and more too, why is not the self co-extensive with the universe?

Now, this is exactly what it is. The self is co-extensive with the universe. The difference between organic beings is merely how much of themselves they realize. The separate personality is real only in terms of matter and in such forms of consciousness as originate or are expressed in terms of material existence.

The self is believed to be a separate entity only because of the overwhelming preponderance in human life of sensory experience, which through habit, fostered by natural selection, tends to impose its laws on all human consciousness. This is the fundamental fact of human life. Consciousness is continuous and universal. Matter is separate and particular. But we habitually think in terms of matter. In short, we live in terms of matter. It is only on those terms that we live at all. If we deviate from them in the slightest degree, our earthly career is promptly terminated by the simple law of natural selection, the survival of the fittest to survive.

Each man therefore carries in himself the conditions and limitations of his own universe, and it is for him to say how large that universe shall be. Habitual actions always tend to become reflex, and the more attention he pays to his own separate material existence, the more restricted his universe becomes. It is a tautology to say that attention to individual physical needs, physical sensations, and the centripetal reflexes growing from them, tends to perpetuate and insure physical existence. On the other hand, everything that tends away from self, such as unselfish love, parental love, and the altruistic centrifugal reflexes developed from them, tends to expansion; and the larger the included circle of altruistic action is, the smaller the danger becomes of perpetuating the restrictions of separate individual existence imposed by natural selection acting in and through the material world.

This conflict of the centripetal and centrifugal forces, of which the so-called self is the centre, is the basis of morality. Broadly speaking, what is done for one's self is bad; what is done for some one else is good. Consciously or unconsciously, this idea lies at the foundation of all the highest moral teaching. The highest virtues are those that conduce to the extinction of terrestrial types. The struggle for existence is the struggle for terrestrial, that is, material existence. If a selfish man and an altruist are wrecked on a desert island with only food enough for one, the selfish man will survive. The penalty of altruism is extermination. Yet no one would maintain for a moment that the altruist is not the higher type of man.

If I have been so fortunate as to make the subject clear up to this point, you will understand that the material self is the fixed point from which man is measured. To expand the consciousness away from it means spiritual growth. To contract toward it means spiritual deterioration. To work away from it means, in familiar language, virtue; to work toward it, vice.

To work toward it requires no effort whatever. A man has only to let himself go, to make himself passive to the law of the survival of the fittest, and he drops there as naturally as a stone falls, if he is dominated, as most men are, by the lower reflexes. The upper altruistic reflexes will eventually carry him the other way as they become strong enough. But the commonest condition of the human race is the natural passive tendency to gravitate to the centre, on the one hand, opposed by the active force of the will and of whatever higher reflexes a man may have, on the other. As before, we come back to the will as the determinant factor.

If you have followed me so far, you will follow me a step further. If a man consists of states of consciousness, as the Buddhist doctrine affirms, then so far as any of them cease, the man ceases. So far as any of them last, the man lasts, and lasts as long as they do, and no longer.

Have we any evidence on how long they last?

A good deal. Let us take *a priori* evidence first. Those qualities, said Darwin, that have been longest inherited are surest to be inherited. And the same is true of the states of consciousness. Those which are formed most slowly dissolve most slowly.

Sensory impressions come in a perpetual shower, and the drops for the most part dry as soon as they fall. Ninety-nine hundredths of our sensory impressions are transitory. Most of them do not call for action of any sort, any more than the passing landscape seen from a car window.

But certain ones do call for action; and if they are repeated often enough, that action becomes first habitual, then reflex or automatic, and any further stimulus of the same sort tends to be dealt with primarily by that habitual reflex, and only secondarily by the consciousness and will. Now it is the sum of a number of such habitual reflexes acting singly or together that we call character. It may be changed—it is changed more or less — during an ordinary life, but it is part of the makeup of every individual at birth. Where does it come from? From the parents?

The fact of the resemblance of offspring to parents is a matter of everyday knowledge all over the world. In the West we call it an illustration of heredity or atavism, the persistence of a parental or ancestral type. In the East it is regarded as an illustration of rebirth or reincarnation. There is no mystery about it. There is no disagreement in regard to the facts. The West, talking in general colloquial terms of body and soul, regards the body inherited from the parents—that is, the physical and material body — as the determinant factor, the mould to which all non-physical qualities necessarily conform, because they are in some way produced by or derived from it.

The East, on the other hand, regarding the collection of qualities familiarly expressed by the term "soul" as dominant, says that a soul has renewed its relations with the material world by rebirth, and gradually, in the process of normal growth, has forced the matter with which it is associated into more or less the same shape that it had before, just as the seed in the course of normal growth forces the inorganic

matter of the air and soil into the shape
of the plant from which it came. In
Japanese the process is habitually
known and spoken of by this resemblance. The Japanese word for it is
INGWA, IN meaning seed and KWA
flower. Of late years in the West the
Sanscrit word KARMA has come to
be somewhat loosely used with the
same general meaning, though some
of the highest Buddhist authorities in
Japan are inclined to restrict the meaning of Karma to one element of the
process.

It is beyond my scope to-night to
draw comparisons or present argu-
ments. My business is simply to state
the facts as they appear from the Buddhist standpoint. But I cannot help
calling attention to one or two points

bearing on the general problem of heredity versus rebirth : —

First. If material constitution, that is, inheritance, which makes for identity, modified by the tendency to variation, is the cause of character, then, as the laws of matter do not vary, we have no way of accounting for the tendency to variation itself. It is an unknown x, an ultimate fact with nothing behind it.

Whereas, if the psychical characteristics — the soul, to take the shortest word — are the dominant factor, the tendency to variation follows as a matter of course.

Second. If material constitution is the cause of character, the range of variation ought to be equally great in different forms of animal life; for instance, in men, sheep, and herring. Whereas, if the variation is determined by the character, we ought to find the greatest variation where the characters are most complex,—which we do.

Third. Family resemblance often asserts itself most clearly in the second generation. And it will be noticed that the very close resemblance of a child to a grandparent is generally associated with two facts,—one, that the ancestor in question has been dead less than ten years; the other, that the very marked resemblance occurs but once, no matter how numerous the grandchildren may be. Heredity by physical transmission offers no explanation of either fact. Whereas, from three to ten years is the ordinary interval for reincarnation, and the single resemblance is the natural result of the rebirth of a single soul.

The apparent bearing of Mendel's law here is too obvious to be overlooked. But it is perhaps too early to be sure just what is behind Mendel's law.

Now, if character reincarnates, what becomes of it between whiles, between the time of one man's death and the next man's birth?

Let me remind you of Darwin again. "Those characteristics are most sure to be transmitted which have been longest transmitted." But as I have tried to show you, character is built up of reflexes which are essentially and necessarily the oldest things about the individual organism. Therefore, according to Darwin, the character is exactly what we should expect to find transmitted.

But this does not answer the question of what becomes of it in the interval between death and birth. A living man's character we know, but a dead body has no character. If that character persists, it must be somewhere in the mean time. There is a gap here to be filled up.

Is there?

Let me ask you to recall that subject of breakfast. Remember that no consciousness but immediate sensory consciousness is conditioned by space and time. Remember that immediate sensory consciousness depends on the action of the matter of the external universe on the matter of the body, and stops at death. And then consider

the question of what has become of
the reincarnating entity in the interval.
From the point of view of that entity
the interval as we know it does not
exist, and it is our error to suppose
that it does,—an error arising as usual
from our disastrous habit of thinking
in terms based on matter.

Is, then, rebirth in one's own family
the only alternative?

By no means. The soul follows its
strongest ties. These are generally the
family ties, but not always; and the
soul always finds its own level where
its own character is most at home. If
it is too sensual and self-absorbed, that
is, too centripetal, to find a human
birth at all, it will find its birth as an
animal; and if it is not only too self-
centred but too actively hostile to

everything outside itself to find a birth even as an animal, it will be born lower still.

On the other hand, if its main trait is centrifugal and altruistic, it will be born where those qualities have fullest play in a higher state of existence.

This higher state is mainly altruistic. The animal kingdom is mainly selfish. Human life is partly one and partly the other.

Now, a word in conclusion about the material environment and incidents of a given life. I have said that conscious-ness is continuous. That means you cannot, so to speak, pick up a single idea alone any more than you can pick up a single knot in the middle of a fish-net. You may pick up any knot you like, but you will get also what

is tied to it. And if, at any point of
the summed-up consciousness of a
man's life, there is tied the record of
an injury done to another man, that
record will infallibly remain tied; and
when, in a later life, in disentangling the
threads of his own existence in terms
of time and space, he comes again to
that particular point, that injury will
return against him with the accuracy
of a spring which expends when re-
leased the exact energy required to com-
press it, and the blow he receives will
be just as hard as the blow he gave.
Action and reaction are equal and
opposite.

From a higher point of view the
case may be put in this way. Consciousness is continuous. Therefore,
there is but one ultimate conscious-

ness. All beings are therefore one; and when one man strikes another, he strikes all men, including himself. Just when and where and how in terms of space and time he feels his own blow depends on circumstances, but sooner or later he will. A good deed comes back to the doer in just the same way.

I just said that consciousness is one, and all beings are therefore one. The difference in beings, therefore, is how much they realize of this universal consciousness. The process of evolution is the process of increase of the amount realized. The only thing that prevents a man from realizing the whole of it is the accumulated habit of countless generations of thinking in terms of self, that is, of the material self. It was not the fault of our

struggling predecessors on this planet
that they thought in these terms. Natural selection took care of that. They
had to, or die.

This universal consciousness is what
all existence started from and is re-
turning to. How easily it can be reached
by organized beings depends on their
place in the scale of evolution. The
fish is farther from it than the dog,
and the dog farther than we, and we
farther than higher beings. The important thing to us is that, having
evolved to the stage of human beings
on our road to it, we can now see
where we are going, and can greatly
increase our speed if we like.

There are two ways in which this
may be done. Character, as I have so
often said, is habitual consciousness;

and I have compared the consciousness, that is, the man, to the dial of a watch that registers either the movement of external nature or the impulse of the will. The two ways of growth correspond to this. In Buddhism they are called respectively the Objective or Exterior and the Subjective or Interior Methods or Systems.[1]

One is through the external acts of daily life, by so ordering them that the lower reflexes are gradually eliminated and the higher ones left and developed. In other words, by doing good actions.

The other is internal, through the

[1] In Japanese *Kengyo* and *Mikkyo*, literally, "Apparent" and "Non-apparent Systems." Occasional erroneous translation of these terms as "Revealed" and "Secret or Esoteric Doctrine" has led to some popular misconceptions.

alteration of the character and consciousness by the direct action of the will.

The first involves the simple practice of ordinary morality. It is safe and sure, and for people occupied with the ordinary affairs of life, usually the best. The character is gradually altered, just as it was built up, by contact with the external world. The ordinary process of evolutionary growth is accelerated, but there is no break in it.

The second way equally involves the practice of morality in daily life. In addition, it involves the direct action of the will on the character. It is generally difficult, and except for people of thoroughly good character, or under the guidance of people of thoroughly good character, liable to be dangerous.

The reason is obvious. In most people
the character, especially in the lower
reflexes, is stronger than the will, even
when the will does not habitually aid
and abet them. In a direct conflict between will and character, the character
is apt to get the upper hand. I have
spoken of the external material universe as a sort of pendulum or balance
wheel to the organism. In the present
case the simile is exact. It goes at a
certain rate, and keeps the delicate
machinery of the human consciousness from deviating very far from that
rate. It limits, to a certain extent, the
amount of good or harm a man can
do to other men and consequently to
himself. But if the balance wheel is
disconnected even temporarily, as in
meditation, the first tendency of the

clock is to obey the pressure of the
mainspring, and run down violently
and perhaps disastrously. If we try to
check this pressure with the key, we
hold it in very unstable equilibrium.
And if we try with the key to make
the hands go at any even rate, it is
almost impossible.

Now, the spring is the character,
and the key is the will, and if the character is bad, the result is disastrous,
because in most people, as I have repeated so often, natural selection has
made the lower reflexes strongest, and
it is consequently those that come into
play first.

Such exercise of the will acting directly on the character has two effects :
It expands the consciousness, and
solidifies the character by strength-

ening the reflexes. But if the consciousness is expanded and the reflexes are strengthened in the direction
of matter, the clock-hands are going
round the wrong way, and the second
state of the man is worse than the
first.

The ultimate object of life is to
acquire freedom from the limitations
of the material world by substituting
volitional for sensory consciousness.
They are limitations to be outgrown.
There is a story of the last century
that Emerson was stopped in the
street by an excited member of the
now forgotten sect of Millerites, who
exclaimed, " Mr. Emerson, do you
know that the world is going to be
destroyed in ten days?" "Well,"
said Emerson, " I don't see but we

shall get along just as well without it."

That is good Buddhist doctrine.

The next step — the next step of
the human race — is to learn how, as
Emerson says, to get along without
it, and without the limitations of
thought that long contact with it has
engendered. They are very hard to
shake off. Even our ideas, — I use
the plural advisedly, for hardly any
two people agree completely, — our
ideas of the highest possible state
of existence are generally anthropomorphic, and based on the familiar
experience of daily life. We imagine
ourselves celestial beings with celestial bodies, but those bodies have a
close resemblance to our own.

Such beings, if we may trust the

highest authorities, have the aspect
of human beings. They have arms
and legs and eyes and ears, noses
and mouths, and none of these or-
gans appear to be atrophied from
disuse. Their pleasures may be more
refined than ours and more in-
tense, their bodies of finer matter
than ours; but they are still separate
individuals, and in so far forth their
existence is governed by the laws of
separation, which are the laws of matter. The distinctions of subject and
object, of ego and non-ego, of external and internal, of active and passive, still hold good, and such beings
live under the same laws of action
and reaction and interaction that gov-
ern us. The highest form of happi-
ness we can conceive for them is

expressed in expanded terms of our
own lives, in an inexhaustible oppor-
tunity for the satisfaction of an inexhaustible desire, whether for work or
play or worship.

Such glorified celestial existence is
the final goal of most religions. In
Northern Buddhism it is not the goal,
but an intermediate step in normal
evolution between the human consciousness and the infinite consciousness, and the difference between these
is as great as that between the dimensions of the material physical body and
the whole physical universe.

You are all more or less familiar
with that extraordinary entity upon
whose inferential existence the lines
of modern scientific research seem to
converge, the interstellar ether, which

seems likely to prove the ultimate form of matter out of which everything comes and into which everything must eventually return. You know the seemingly contradictory qualities that the hypothesis of its existence involves, — how it is perfectly rigid and perfectly elastic, perfectly dense and perfectly penetrable, hot and cold, heavy and light, and so on as far as we like to go. But, as I have said, antinomies cannot condition existence; and all this simply means that the ether is unconditioned, an entity of no properties but of all possibilities, or, more exactly, not an entity at all, but an infinite possibility.

To our minds it may serve as a symbol of an idea we cannot well grasp without a symbol, the idea of unconditioned consciousness.

From this the universe has come. To this the universe and everything in it returns. We have come a long way up the scale of evolution guided by natural selection. We have come to the point where we can begin to do our own selecting. We can understand something of the rules of the game, and see something of the board in our immediate neighborhood, although our consciousness is so cramped and shriveled and atrophied by long contact with the limitations of material existence that we can barely and dimly realize the immensity of that which is at once our origin and our goal.

But we have our choice. It is not

the world, but the universe, that is all before us where to choose. We may take as much or as little of it as we like. We may take the smallest part or the whole. But only the whole is free. The parts are conditioned by relations with space and time and each other, and if we choose a part, we must take with it the adjoining connected parts. That is the price. The Hindus have long since put this into a popular saying, —"What will you have?" said God to man. "Take it, and pay for it."

But the choice is ours. You remember how well Emerson has said this in that great poem called "Days," that begins —

"Daughters of Time, the hypocritic Days,
Muffled and dumb like barefoot dervishes,

And marching single in an endless file,
Bring diadems and fagots in their hands.
To each they offer gifts after his will,
Bread, kingdoms, stars, and sky that holds them
    all.''

Never, perhaps, has the choice been better stated. Bread, the symbol of the evanescent needs of daily physical life; kingdoms, of power; the stars, of the highest knowledge of material things; and the sky that holds them all, of the last and greatest alternative, the ultimate expansion of consciousness that knows neither limit nor boundary. Only in this expanded consciousness is the will free. Only in limited forms is its freedom hampered. The so-called necessity that seems to oppose it is made up of the limitations of personality and material existence.

There is a Japanese proverb that says, "There are many roads up the mountain, but it is always the same moon that is seen from the top." The Japanese themselves, with a liberality worthy of imitation, apply this saying to different forms of religious belief. The mountain may well typify matter, and the summit the highest accessible point on which a climber can stand and maintain his separate individual existence in terms of consciousness drawn from the material world. This peak may be accessible by any religion, or without any religion; but Buddhism and its genetically associated systems look beyond. The mountain top is the apotheosis of personal existence, the highest form of consciousness that can be expressed in terms of separate individuality, — a sublime elevation, where many a pilgrim is content to pause. Below him are the kingdoms; above him are the stars; and kingdoms and stars alike are his. But it is not the end. Deeper than the kingdoms, and higher than the stars, is the sky that holds them all. And there alone is peace, — that peace that the material world cannot give, — the peace that passeth understanding trained on material things, — infinite and eternal peace, — the peace of limitless consciousness unified with limitless will.

That peace is NIRVANA.

CPSIA information can be obtained
at www.ICGtesting.com
Printed in the USA
BVHW04s1933160818
524748BV00006B/55/P

9 781375 409254